★ IT'S MY STATE! ★

PUERTO RICO

Ruth Bjorklund

Richard Hantula

Cavendish
Square

New York

Published in 2014 by Cavendish Square Publishing, LLC
303 Park Avenue South, Suite 1247, New York, NY 10010

Library of Congress Cataloging-in-Publication Data
Bjorklund, Ruth.
        Puerto Rico / Ruth Bjorklund and Richard Hantula.—2nd ed.
            p. cm.—(It's my state!)
        Includes bibliographical references and index.
        Summary: "Surveys the history, geography, government, economy, and people of Puerto Rico"—Provided by publisher.
        ISBN 978-1-60870-883-3 (hardcover)—978-1-62712-096-8 (paperback)—ISBN 978-1-60870-889-5 (ebook)
        1. Puerto Rico—Juvenile literature. I. Hantula, Richard. II. Title.
    F1958.3.B56 2013
    972.95—dc23   2012005179

This edition developed for Cavendish Square Publishing by RJF Publishing LLC (www.RJFpublishing.com)
Series Designer, Second Edition: Tammy West/Westgraphix LLC

All maps, illustrations, and graphics © Cavendish Square Publishing, LLC. Maps and artwork on pages 6, 42, 43, 74, 75 and back cover by Christopher Santoro. Map and graphics on pages 8 and 47 by Westgraphix LLC.

Printed in the United States of America

PUERTO RICO

CONTENTS

Official Flower: Puerto Rican Hibiscus

The Puerto Rican hibiscus is a large hibiscus-like blossom. Not a true hibiscus, it is the flower of the *maga* tree. All year round, the tree's branches are covered with shiny green leaves. The wood of the maga tree is highly prized and used in making musical instruments and furniture.

Official Bird: Puerto Rican Spindalis

This bird lives in forests and plantations, where it feasts chiefly on fruits and berries. The male has green and yellow markings, with a black-and-white striped head. The female has fainter markings.

Official Tree: Ceiba

The ceiba, or kapok tree, is one of several so-called silk-cotton trees. It grows rapidly, reaching heights of 150 feet (45 meters) or more. It has white or pink flowers, and the fruit is a pod filled with seeds and with a cotton-like fiber. The trunk was once used by native Taino people to craft giant dugout canoes. Ceiba seeds are processed to make cooking oil and soap.

Common Fish: Parrot Fish

The parrot fish was given its name because its mouth resembles a parrot's beak and its scales are bright shades of red, yellow, green, and blue. The mouth of a parrot fish is filled with tiny teeth, which it uses to scrape off and feed on algae and other living things that cling to rocks and coral. Parrot fish range in length from about 8 inches (20 centimeters) to 5 feet (1.5 m) or so. They live in warm shallow water and sleep at night hidden between rocks.

Common Mammal: Mongoose

In 1877, sugarcane growers brought the mongoose from Southeast Asia to control rats that fed on sugarcane. Mongooses range in length from 10 to 25 inches (25 to 63 cm) and can weigh from 1 pound to 30 pounds (0.5 to 14 kilograms). These long, brownish-gray mammals are successful predators due to their quick climbing and running. Their varied diet of rats, frogs, insects, snakes, birds, and fruits has contributed to an explosion of their numbers in Puerto Rico. They are now considered pests.

Common Amphibian: Coqui

The coqui (pronounced "ko-KEE") is a tiny tree frog that lives throughout Puerto Rico and has become an unofficial symbol of the commonwealth. In fact, when Puerto Ricans want to describe their nationality, many use the expression *Soy de aquí como el coquí* ("I am from here like the coqui"). At night, coquis climb trees, and the male frogs noisily chirp "ko-KEE, ko-KEE." Some forests are home to 10,000 coquis per acre (0.4 hectare), and their chirping can be deafening. Unlike most frogs, coquis hatch as miniature frogs and not as tadpoles.

PUERTO RICO

ATLANTIC OCEAN

ISLA DESECHEO

ISLA MONITO

MONA PASSAGE

ISLA MONA

Aquadilla

Isabela

GUAJATACA FOREST

RÍO GRANDE de AÑASCO

ARECIBO OBSERVATORY

RÍO ARECIBO

Arecibo

VEGA ALTA FOREST

Vega Baja

RÍO GRANDE de MANATÍ

RÍO LA PLATA

San Juan

Río Grande

EL YUNQUE FOREST

ISLA CULEBRA

Ceiba

Cabo Rojo

Adjuntas

CERRO de PUNTA

TORO NEGRO FOREST

RÍO LOIZA

ISLA VIEQUES

VIEQUES SOUND

CORDILLERA CENTRAL

Caguas

Yabucoa

GUÁNICA FOREST RESERVE

Yauco

Ponce

Santa Isabel

ISLA CAJA de MUERTOS

CARIBBEAN SEA

N

W — E

S

Isle of Enchantment

Nineteenth-century Puerto Rican poet José Gautier Benítez called his homeland *un jardín encantado*, which means "an enchanted garden." In his day, Puerto Rico was a sleepy, semitropical island bursting with exotic trees, flowers, fruits, birds, and fish. Today, much has changed. The island now bustles with modern activities. Yet, as gardens bloom, seas sparkle, and rain forests shine, Puerto Ricans are still proud to call their home an "isle of enchantment."

Its capital, San Juan, is an old town, founded in the sixteenth century. Unlike most U.S. states, Puerto Rico is not divided into counties. Instead, it is composed of seventy-eight *municipios*, or municipalities. The municipios are divided into neighborhoods called barrios. San Juan, where some 400,000 people live, is the municipio with the largest population.

Seas, Mountains, and More

Puerto Rico is a commonwealth, a self-governing unit tied to the United States. The commonwealth consists of a main island and several smaller islands, with a total land area of 3,424 square miles (8,868 square kilometers). It is the most easterly part of an island chain called the Greater

Quick Facts

PUERTO RICO BORDERS

North	Atlantic Ocean
South	Caribbean Sea
East	Caribbean Sea
West	Mona Passage

Puerto Rico has 78 municipios.

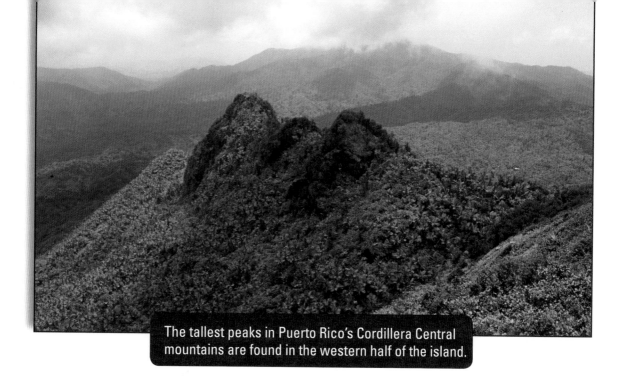

The tallest peaks in Puerto Rico's Cordillera Central mountains are found in the western half of the island.

Antilles. The main island of Puerto Rico is almost rectangular in shape. It measures about 111 miles (179 km) east to west and 36 miles (58 km) north to south.

Vieques, Culebra, and several small islets lie to the east of the main island. Mona and other, smaller islets lie to the west. Islets to the south include Caja de Muertos, a nature reserve. The commonwealth lies more than 1,000 miles (1,600 km) southeast of Miami, Florida, 500 miles (800 km) north of Venezuela in South America, and 70 miles (100 km) east of the Dominican Republic, from which it is separated by a stretch of sea called the Mona Passage.

Although Puerto Rico is small in size—just a bit larger than Rhode Island and Delaware combined—it has a wide and colorful variety of plants and animals. There are many types of terrain—from ocean beaches to mountains—and a range of weather patterns. The main island is divided east to west across its center by high mountains called the Cordillera Central.

Quick Facts

DEEP WATER
The Puerto Rico Trench contains the deepest part of the Atlantic Ocean. The deepest point of the trench lies about 100 miles (160 km) northwest of Puerto Rico. It is more than 5 miles (8 km) below sea level.

Over many centuries, the waters of Río Camuy carved hundreds of caves in the northwestern part of the main island. Some of these caves are open to visitors.

The island's highest peak, Cerro de Punta, which rises to 4,390 feet (1,338 m), is located there. Approximately fifty rivers run off the mountains toward the sea, many flowing through green and fertile valleys.

Thanks to winds from the Atlantic Ocean that blow frequent rainstorms ashore, the northeastern part of the main island is especially lush and green. A mountain range called the Sierra de Luquillo rises there. One of its highest peaks is called El Yunque. This same name, El Yunque, is also given to Puerto Rico's national forest. That forest is the only tropical rain forest in the U.S. national forest system. El Yunque is dense with fascinating plants such as giant ferns, orchids, mahogany trees, and bamboo. Some of its plants are not found on the U.S. mainland.

The landscape of the northwestern part of Puerto Rico's main island is unlike the northeastern region. In the northwest, many of the rivers run underground for part of their course. One of them, Río Camuy, forms the third-largest underground river in the world. Much of the land in the northwest is made of limestone. Over time, the rivers, wind, and rainfall have eroded the limestone into dramatic caverns, caves, trenches, and towering cone-shaped hills. This type of geographic area is known as karst.

Weather affects each side of the island differently. Like many islands, the main island has a windier, stormier side, called the windward side. The calmer protected side is called the leeward side. The windward part of the main island is on the north side. It receives nearly twice as much rainfall as the southern, leeward side of the island. The southwestern part is particularly dry. Cacti and other plants that grow under dry conditions thrive in this region. Here, in the dry season of November to April, leaves fall from many of the trees.

For many people, the most popular places in Puerto Rico are the soft-sand coastal beaches that encircle the island. Palm trees, pineapple plants, citrus trees, and other tropical plants grow throughout the nearby coastal plains. Lagoons, which are saltwater and freshwater ponds that lie separated from the sea by sandbars or reefs, dot the shoreline. So do mangrove trees, which thrive along lagoons. Puerto Rico also has coral reefs. Coral reefs are living structures made up of the external skeletons of tiny animals called corals bound together by calcium and other deposits. Coral reefs provide a rich habitat for sea life along the south and west coastlines.

Of the outer islands, Vieques is the largest and most populated. It is green and hilly with wide, sandy beaches. Culebra and Mona islands also have wide beaches, but both are quite dry, featuring rocks, cliffs, and cacti. Forests and grasslands are also found on Culebra. Part of the island along with neighboring islets form the Culebra National Wildlife Refuge. The entire island of Mona is a wildlife refuge.

Climate

Puerto Rico lies in an area of the world known as the tropics. This zone stretches in a band around Earth at its equator. The tropics receive the same amount of daylight in the winter and in the summer because the sun stays in the same position directly over the equator every day. The tropics can be quite hot.

However, since Puerto Rico faces the Atlantic Ocean, where cooling ocean breezes blow, Puerto Rico enjoys relatively moderate temperatures. Year-round, the temperature barely changes, ranging on average from 74 degrees Fahrenheit (23 degrees Celsius) in winter months to 81 °F (27 °C) in the summer. Coasts of the main island are usually warmer than interior areas, where the temperature typically averages between 73 °F and 78 °F (23 °C and 26 °C). The south tends to be warmer than the north. The coolest temperatures are found in the mountains.

Puerto Rico's coastal beaches enjoy sunshine and warm temperatures year-round.

Hurricane Georges struck Puerto Rico in September 1998 with wind speeds up to 115 miles (185 km) per hour. The storm caused widespread damage and several deaths.

Puerto Ricans are quick to point out that barely a day goes by without sunshine. This is true for most areas. However, the northern coast of the main island receives frequent rain brought on by steady winds from the Atlantic. Whenever storm clouds push against the mountains, it is a sure bet that it will rain on this part of the island. Rainfall in parts of El Yunque National Forest, for example, can reach more than 250 inches (630 cm) a year. But in the crowded coastal areas, annual rainfall may be 60 inches (150 cm) or more in the north and below 35 to 40 inches (90 to 100 cm) in the south. November through April are the drier, slightly cooler months. May through October are the rainy months, during which time the average temperatures are a few degrees warmer.

Although Puerto Rico's climate is generally warm and pleasant, sometimes weather conditions can turn dangerous. This occurs most often during hurricane season. According to the U.S. National Weather Service, hurricane season lasts from June 1 to November 30. Hurricanes are intense tropical storms that produce heavy rains and wind speeds of at least 74 miles (119 km) per hour. Hurricanes do not strike Puerto Rico every year. But when they occur, they can be destructive.

A hurricane with sustained wind speeds greater than 155 miles (249 km) per hour struck in 1928. Known as Hurricane San Felipe II, it killed 300 people. Most hurricanes that affect Puerto Rico are not so ferocious. But they can still cause a great deal of damage. In 2011, Hurricane Irene produced widespread flooding and left more than 1 million people without electric power.

Island Creatures

Bats, manatees, whales, and dolphins are the only native wild mammals in the region. Few other mammals are found in Puerto Rico. They were generally brought by or came with humans. Mongooses, for example, thrive in the forests but are not native to the islands. They were introduced in 1877 to control rats—which had come to Puerto Rico as stowaways on ships. Some rhesus and squirrel monkeys that were brought for research purposes escaped into the wild and have flourished in the tropical climate. On the island of Mona, pigs and goats, brought by humans long ago, run wild.

Many reptiles and amphibians can be found in Puerto Rico. There are several types of snakes, though only one is thought to be poisonous, the Puerto Rican racer. Lizards, such as anoles and geckos, lurk everywhere—in forests, beaches, and cities. They range in size from the tiny Monito gecko, at a mere 1.5 inches (4 cm), to the Mona ground iguana, which can grow to more than 4 feet (1 m) in length (including tail). Both are considered endangered—that is, at risk of dying out. Also endangered

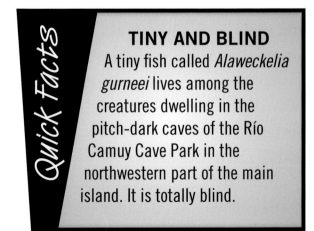

TINY AND BLIND
A tiny fish called *Alaweckelia gurneei* lives among the creatures dwelling in the pitch-dark caves of the Río Camuy Cave Park in the northwestern part of the main island. It is totally blind.

Quick Facts

Several types of sea turtles can be found in the waters around Puerto Rico.

are four different types of sea turtles: hawksbill, leatherback, loggerhead, and green. These creatures live most of their life in the open sea. They come ashore only to lay their eggs in the sand. Sea turtles have been hunted for their meat, eggs, or shells. Well over a dozen types of frogs live in Puerto Rico. The one most Puerto Ricans are familiar with is the coqui, a tiny brownish frog that sings its distinctive song all night long.

Marine life is abundant in the waters around Puerto Rico. Some areas of the ocean are very deep, while others are shallow and contain coral reefs. Corals need warm, clear, shallow water to survive. They also need wave action or currents to wash in food. Coral reefs provide an environment for many other kinds of marine life. In the coral reefs around Puerto Rico, there are sponges, sea anemones, octopuses, lobsters, conchs, angelfish, parrot fish, red snappers, tuna, and

BIRD-WATCHER'S PARADISE

The Guánica State Forest covers an area of 9,900 acres (4,000 ha) and is the world's largest tropical dry coastal forest. Noted for its diversity of species, especially of birds, it has been recognized as a biosphere reserve by the United Nations.

Bird-watchers may spot some types of birds in the Guánica State Forest that have become rare in other areas.

dolphins. Mosquito Bay on Vieques and two other bays in Puerto Rico are known for tiny organisms called dinoflagellates. At night, these creatures emit an eerie light, causing the water in the bay to glow.

Insects and spiders thrive in Puerto Rico. There are dozens of species, or types, of spiders, many of which are harmless. But some carry strong venom, including the black widow spider, the tarantula, and a wolf spider that may eat even small frogs and lizards. There are also more than 5,000 species of insects. Common types include mosquitoes, flies, termites, grasshoppers, dragonflies, beetles, and butterflies.

Many of Puerto Rico's 350 species of birds feast on the plentiful insects. The Guánica State Forest, a dry forest (that is, a forest marked by a long dry season) in the southwestern part of the main island, is host to many types of birds. They include migratory birds such as egrets, herons, ibises, and todies, as well as such native birds as the Puerto Rican lizard cuckoo and the Puerto Rican nightjar. Along the coast, seabirds gather. They include grebes, tropic birds, pelicans, terns, boobies, bitterns, ducks, plovers, laughing gulls, and frigate birds. In the forests live hummingbirds, falcons, hawks, screech owls, tanagers, canaries, parakeets, mockingbirds, and doves.

Puerto Rico's most treasured natural region is El Yunque National Forest. It features one of the most diverse environments in the world. Its 28,000 acres (11,300 ha) contain 240 types of trees, 150 types of ferns, and 50 varieties of orchids. The forest also is the home of animals such as the rare Puerto Rican parrot. Environmentalists and concerned citizens are working to preserve this remarkable rain forest. They do not want to see it developed—turned into cropland or pasture for grazing animals.

The land that is now El Yunque National Forest was first set aside as a protected area in the late 1800s, to preserve its diversity of plants and animals.

Ghost-Faced Bat

Bats are the most common mammals in Puerto Rico. One kind of bat, the ghost-faced bat, is small and reddish-brown, with unusual folds of skin across its face. It hangs by two legs and lives in caves. At sunset, the animal leaves its cave and feeds on insects, capturing them while flying.

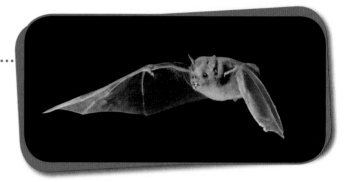

Mangrove

Mangrove trees grow in salty wetlands along coastlines. They breathe oxygen through their roots. Their extensive root system gives shelter to small fish, shellfish, and crocodiles. As the roots thicken and collect soil around them, mangroves protect shorelines from damage due to floods, tides, and storms.

Puerto Rican Parrot

The Puerto Rican parrot, with its large head and brilliant green and blue feathers, is one of the rarest creatures on Earth. Once plentiful, these parrots now number fewer than fifty in the wild. The birds have become endangered mostly because of hunting and destruction of their native forest habitat. Environmentalists are working to raise parrots in captivity and release them into the wild to increase their numbers.

Flamboyant Tree

The flamboyant tree, also called the flame tree, is not native to Puerto Rico but is very popular. Its colorful flowers and bright green leaves make a striking sight in the countryside. The town of Peñuelas on the south coast is known as "The Valley of the Flamboyant Trees."

Leatherback Sea Turtle

The leatherback sea turtle is the world's largest turtle. It also dives the deepest and stays under water the longest. Unlike other turtles, the leatherback has a rubbery shell. Like other sea turtles, leatherbacks are endangered. They are often caught in fish nets and drown. They also are disturbed by passing boats, and some choke on floating plastic garbage.

Puerto Rican Lizard Cuckoo

The Puerto Rican lizard cuckoo is found only in Puerto Rico, living in the island's forests, woodlands, and plantation fields. The cuckoos are colorful birds with long tails and curved bills. They are secretive and move slowly, flying in a straight line while looking for prey. The island's many lizards are their preferred food. The cuckoo can imitate many of the sounds it hears.

From the Beginning

Over many centuries, people from all over the world have landed on Puerto Rico's shores. Most historians agree that people first arrived on the islands of the Caribbean, including present-day Puerto Rico, much later than on the nearby continents of North and South America. Many experts believe that by around 2000 BCE, people from the Orinoco region of what is now Venezuela were living in the region of today's Puerto Rico. People originally from the area of today's Yucatán Peninsula (Mexico) and the Central American country of Belize may also have come to the Puerto Rico region. Little trace is left of such early peoples.

After approximately 500 BCE, the Saladoid people—probably from South America—dominated the region for hundreds of years. They were good farmers and pottery makers. Scientists today learn about them by studying objects they made.

By 1200 CE, a people called the Tainos were living in the region. Scientists are not sure whether the Tainos were descended from earlier groups in the area or came by sea from elsewhere. The Tainos had their own name for what is now Puerto Rico. They called their land Borinquen, meaning "Land of the Noble (or Valiant) Lord."

The Taino people were peaceful. They were also expert sailors, fishers, and woodworkers who, with stone tools, carved seaworthy dugout canoes from whole

The Tainos created petroglyphs, which are artworks carved or drawn on rock.

ceiba trees. They built well-planned villages. Chiefs, called *caciques*, lived in rectangular houses made of wood and straw, while workers lived in round huts. The Tainos' buildings all faced a common area called a *batey*, where ceremonies and games were held. For food, the Tainos fished and hunted birds, iguanas, and sea turtles. To add to their food supply, they farmed crops, such as yucca (cassava), maize (corn), beans, squash, sweet potatoes, pineapples, and peppers. The Tainos also grew cotton and wove its fibers into cloth, as well as nets and sleeping hammocks. Both men and women wore decorations of paint on their bodies, as well as shell bracelets and jewelry such as gold earrings, nose rings, and necklaces.

Spanish Rule

In 1493, the Italian-born sea captain Christopher Columbus sailed from Spain to colonize lands in the New World, which he had visited on a voyage the year before. It was on this second voyage that Europeans first arrived on the island of Borinquen. At the time, an estimated 50,000 Tainos were living there.

To the Tainos, Columbus and his men, with their light skin and beards, appeared unlike anyone they had ever seen. They greeted the newcomers with friendliness and awe. Columbus, however, was not interested in making friends.

He was looking for land and wealth for Spain. He gave the island a Spanish name, San Juan Bautista (which is Spanish for Saint John the Baptist, a Christian saint). Over time, the name became shortened to simply San Juan.

Sixteen years later, in 1509, the Spanish explorer and soldier Juan Ponce de León was named the first governor of the island of

Quick Facts

SWEET SOUNDS
Christopher Columbus once wrote that the Tainos spoke the sweetest and most gentle language that he had ever heard. *Taino* as a word means "the good people." Several English words come from the Taino language, including *barbecue, canoe, hammock, hurricane,* and *tobacco.*

San Juan Bautista. His duty was to continue settlement of the island, maintain control over the natives, and extract wealth for Spain. In 1508, Ponce de León had founded a settlement called Caparra close to the northern coast. The town was soon moved to a nearby site on a bay that provided a fine harbor. The new location received the name Puerto Rico (Spanish for "rich port"). A few years later, the town became known as San Juan, and the island came to be called Puerto Rico.

Meanwhile, Spanish priests arrived along with other settlers. King Ferdinand of Spain demanded that the land on the island be divided into large parcels, which he gave to Spanish landowners. The Spaniards forced the Tainos to work for them. The natives were so convinced the Spaniards were as powerful as gods that they did whatever the Spanish people ordered. They worked on Spanish farms, constructed buildings, and mined and processed gold. However, by 1511, a group of Tainos rebelled. The Spaniards put down the revolt, and some of the rebels then fled to the mountains or to neighboring

A statue of Puerto Rico's first Spanish governor, Juan Ponce de León, stands in the city of San Juan.

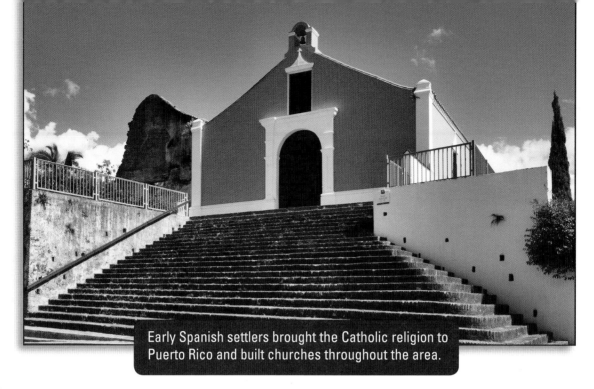

Early Spanish settlers brought the Catholic religion to Puerto Rico and built churches throughout the area.

islands. After the revolt, the Tainos gradually disappeared from the coastal lowlands. Over the years, many of them died from diseases the Europeans had brought. Since the Tainos had never been exposed to the diseases, they had no natural immunity to protect them against becoming sick. In just a few decades, the Tainos' way of life was destroyed.

By 1570, the gold ran out in Puerto Rico. But the Spaniards had found other ways to create wealth. In 1513, Spain officially gave the Spanish people living in Puerto Rico permission to import slaves from Africa. With the labor of African slaves, the Spanish were able to develop large farming operations, called plantations. For a while, their most profitable crop was sugarcane. They grew the tall, grasslike plants and extracted and refined the sugar from them. They shipped the refined sugar to Europe, where it was a prized import. San Juan became a valuable shipping port and a place of power from which Spain could manage its interests and its other lands in the New World.

Spanish engineers built forts in and around San Juan for protection against Spain's enemies. For example, work on a large fort at the entrance to San Juan Bay began in 1539. It was called San Felipe del Morro, honoring Spain's King Felipe (Philip) II. Commonly known as El Morro, it today is one of several fortifications belonging to the San Juan National Historic Site.

Several times, the English and the Dutch attacked Puerto Rico. Usually, Spain was successful in defending its colony. But in 1598, the English took over El Morro and occupied Puerto Rico for several months before an outbreak of disease forced them to leave. Later, in 1625, the Dutch attacked San Juan and burned it. Pirates also attacked from time to time, beginning with an attack in 1528 by French corsairs on the southwestern town of San Germán.

By the late sixteenth century, Puerto Rico was losing its importance as a port for Spanish ships that traded goods between Spain and its New World colonies. Many ships took more direct routes to Latin American territories such as Mexico. Also, Spain demanded that the people of Puerto Rico trade only with it. As a result, fewer ships entered Puerto Rican harbors, and the colony's economy suffered. Spain focused on Puerto Rico's strategic importance. It spent money to improve and maintain fortifications on the island, which it saw as key to protecting its rich territories elsewhere in Latin America.

Meanwhile, planters and small-time Puerto Rican farmers, called *jíbaros*, began planting crops for themselves, not just sugarcane or other crops for Spain. They grew such things as fruits, vegetables, coffee, and tobacco so they could sell them for profit. Despite Spain's restrictions, farmers, businesspeople, and even some government officials began to trade openly with other countries, often with the help of pirates. This illegal trade activity, called smuggling, became widespread. Because of it, the Puerto Rican economy improved.

When the American colonies fought for independence from Great Britain in the American Revolution (1775–1783), Britain barred colonial trading ships from entering any of the ports in its Caribbean colonies. Puerto Rico, belonging to Spain, was open to the colonists' ships. They brought slaves and food, which they traded for Puerto Rican

Quick Facts

SUPER FORT
Not far from El Morro, the Spaniards in 1634 began building a fort called San Cristóbal. In the following century, they enormously expanded it. Covering an area of about 27 acres (11 ha), it was the largest Spanish-built fort in the New World.

UPRISING IN LARES

On September 23, 1868, several hundred people, ranging from slaves to well-off individuals, gathered in the agricultural town of Lares. Armed with machetes and a small number of guns, they declared Puerto Rico an independent republic. The uprising was quickly crushed, but some Puerto Ricans continued to want independence. The uprising is now remembered in Puerto Rican history as El Grito de Lares ("The Shout of Lares").

coffee, tobacco, and molasses. Puerto Rico also provided shelter for colonial ships fleeing from the British.

By the nineteenth century, many Puerto Ricans referred to themselves as criollos. This term once described people of Spanish descent born in Puerto Rico. But it had also come to mean people who were a mixture of the island's cultures—Spanish, African, and Taino. In the 1860s, tensions grew between the criollos and the Spaniards who still controlled the government, most commercial activities, and the military. Although the government made reforms, including the ending of slavery in 1873, many criollos continued to demand more rights. In 1897, Spain agreed to allow Puerto Rico limited autonomy, or self-rule. The island's new government began operation in February of the following year.

The section of Puerto Rico's capital known as Old San Juan still contains many buildings that were put up during Spanish colonial rule.

The United States Takes Over

In April 1898, war broke out between the United States and Spain. U.S. troops invaded the southern shore of the main island on July 25. Less than three weeks later, the two countries stopped fighting, with Spain agreeing to give up its claim to Puerto Rico. A U.S. military governor took control of Puerto Rico on October 18. A peace treaty officially ending the Spanish-American War was signed on December 10 in Paris, France. It awarded Puerto Rico to the United States.

A civil government replaced the military government in Puerto Rico on May 1, 1900. Headed largely by Americans, it had a governor, executive council, and supreme court—all appointed by the U.S. president. The executive council served as the upper house of the legislature. The legislature also had a house of delegates with thirty-five members, elected by local people. Any laws it passed had to be approved by the U.S. Congress. Puerto Rico was allowed an elected representative—called the resident commissioner—in Washington, D.C., but the commissioner, although permitted to speak in Congress, had no vote there. Many Puerto Ricans resented this arrangement. It felt like a return to colonial rule with yet another foreign government controlling the country.

To protest the presence of the United States on the island, the legislature refused to pass any laws in 1909. Then, on March 2, 1917, President Woodrow Wilson signed the Jones Act. This law gave Puerto Ricans the right to U.S. citizenship. It also gave Puerto Ricans some limited personal and civil rights. These included the right to elect the members of both houses of their legislature, which now consisted of a senate with nineteen members and a house of representatives with thirty-nine. One month later, the United States entered World War I, during which more than 18,000 Puerto Ricans served in the U.S. armed forces.

The United States built roads, bridges, schools, dams, and hospitals in Puerto Rico, but some U.S. actions angered many Puerto Ricans. For example, U.S. officials replaced the Puerto Rican peso with the U.S. dollar as the island's currency. Also, in the first decades of the twentieth century, they tried to make English the main language in schools, even though most Puerto Ricans spoke Spanish.

U.S. troops captured the city of Ponce during the Spanish-American War.

While serving in Washington, D.C., as resident commissioner, Luis Muñoz Rivera helped write the Jones Act, giving Puerto Ricans U.S. citizenship.

In the first part of the twentieth century, the sugar industry came to dominate the Puerto Rican economy. But there were problems. Many Puerto Ricans were poor and made a difficult living on small scraps of land. Sugarcane plantation owners, other business leaders, and politicians from the United States held such control over the land that people used the phrase "King Sugar" to describe the wealthy landowners' power. These landowners grew mainly sugarcane, and they made a great deal of money doing so. This left little land for the Puerto Rican people to grow their own crops.

Then, new difficulties arose. Ferocious hurricanes in 1928 and 1932 hurt growers of sugarcane and other major crops. Puerto Rico was hard hit by the Great Depression, a severe economic downturn that affected the United States and many other countries in the 1930s. Poor people struggled to feed and house themselves. Even wealthy people were struggling.

The 1930s also saw the beginning of the political career of Luis Muñoz Marín. A Puerto Rican writer who had studied in the United States, he was the son of Luis Muñoz Rivera, a poet and journalist who had advocated autonomy under Spanish rule and had served as resident commissioner from 1911 to 1916. Luis Muñoz Marín, then a supporter of independence, was elected to the Puerto Rican senate in 1932. In 1938, he helped found the Popular Democratic Party, which sought to improve the lives of the jíbaros and other poor Puerto Ricans. It adopted "Bread, Land, and Liberty" as its slogan. It gained a majority in the Puerto Rican legislature in the 1940 election, and Muñoz Marín became

Workers on sugarcane plantations in the 1930s and early 1940s often received very low pay.

the senate's president. The party went on to keep control of the legislature for twenty-eight years.

The United States entered World War II in 1941. More than 53,000 Puerto Rican men and women served in the U.S. military during the war, which lasted until 1945. Puerto Rico became a key military post for the United States, which established army, navy, and air force bases on the main island and on the smaller islands Culebra and Vieques. The bases provided employment opportunities for Puerto Ricans and helped to attract new industries.

Commonwealth

After the war, Puerto Rico began to gain more control over its own affairs. It received its first native-born governor, Jesús T. Piñero, appointed by President Harry Truman in 1946. The following year, the United States passed a law allowing Puerto Rico to elect its own governor. In 1948, Puerto Rico held its first election for governor. Muñoz Marín won. He pushed for change in Puerto Rico's relationship with the United States. The U.S. Congress agreed to change Puerto

Rico's status to a "free associated state," or commonwealth, with a constitution to be drawn up by the Puerto Ricans. While Muñoz Marín and his followers favored developing such a relationship with the United States, "nationalist" Puerto Ricans wanted full independence. In 1950, some turned to violence, attacking several towns and even attempting to kill Muñoz Marín and Truman. The process of forming a commonwealth continued, however, and in 1952, the new constitution won approval from the U.S. Congress and Puerto Rican voters.

Under its new status Puerto Rico remained subject to the authority of the U.S. president and Congress. However, Puerto Ricans now enjoyed a greater degree of self-rule. They could vote for their own government officials. They remained citizens of the United States, and they continued to use U.S. currency. They did not have to pay federal income taxes, and they could not vote for the U.S. president. As before, they had a representative in Congress—a resident commissioner, belonging to the House of Representatives—but he or she could not vote on legislation.

In addition to his political program, Muñoz Marín pushed for reforms to improve the Puerto Rican economy. Agriculture, long the mainstay of the economy, was shrinking. Muñoz Marín's plan, called Operation Bootstrap, began to take shape before his 1948 election as governor. It used tax breaks and low rents for buildings to attract manufacturing and other industries to Puerto Rico, with the aim of providing good new jobs for Puerto Ricans. By the 1960s, more than 900 plants had been established in Puerto Rico, representing such industries as pharmaceutical (drug) and textile manufacturing. The tourism industry also grew.

Overall, living standards in Puerto Rico were rising. Many local families were earning more money, making it possible for their children to attend colleges and universities. Most people seemed satisfied with the progress. In 1967, a vote was held to determine whether or not Puerto Rico should remain a commonwealth, become a state, or seek independence as a nation. The vote was 60 percent in favor of remaining a commonwealth, 39 percent in favor of statehood, and only 1 percent in favor of becoming an independent nation.

Luis Muñoz Marín helped bring about dramatic changes in Puerto Rico's economy with Operation Bootstrap.

In later years, however, businesses began moving to other countries where labor was cheaper and taxes were lower. Some of those that remained cut jobs. Unemployment would have skyrocketed if not for the fact that some Puerto Ricans moved to the U.S. mainland to find work. They were continuing a migration that began in a small way after the United States took over Puerto Rico. During World War I and World War II, Puerto Ricans who moved or were brought to the mainland served as a valuable source of labor for U.S. industry. An especially large migration occurred in the years after World War II, helped by the growth of air travel. Between 1950 and 1970, for example, 25 to 35 percent of the Puerto Rican population moved to the mainland, according to one estimate.

The Road Ahead

There are mixed opinions about the outlook for Puerto Rico's future. Because of the loss of businesses and industries in recent years, along with pollution problems caused by factories and military bases (now mostly closed), some experts believe the future looks poor. Despite migration to the U.S. mainland, joblessness is high. Puerto Rico was hard hit by the global economic recession that began in late 2007. While the U.S. average unemployment rate in 2010 was 9.6 percent, the figure for Puerto Rico was 16.1 percent.

San Juan's harbor can accommodate even the largest cruise ships, helping make tourism one of Puerto Rico's largest industries.

SONIA SOTOMAYOR

People of Puerto Rican descent play leading roles in all aspects of American life. In 2009, Sonia Sotomayor became the first Hispanic American to serve on the U.S. Supreme Court. Sotomayor, whose parents had moved from Puerto Rico to the mainland during World War II, was born in New York City in 1954. She graduated from Princeton University and Yale University Law School. After working as an assistant district attorney and a lawyer in private practice, she was first appointed a federal judge in 1992. Three years later, she issued a decision, applauded by sports fans, effectively ending a Major League Baseball strike. Sotomayor was serving as a federal appeals court judge when she was named to the Supreme Court by President Barack Obama.

On the other hand, Puerto Ricans tend to be wealthier, healthier, and better educated than most other Caribbean citizens. Some people believe that there is new hope for the island. Sugarcane plantations are no longer a way of life. Farmers have mainly turned to other crops, such as coffee and other tropical foods, and to dairy and livestock farming. The tourism industry is a major source of income. U.S. citizens living in cold, northern states can travel easily to Puerto Rico for a vacation without needing to carry a passport.

Opinions are also mixed about Puerto Rico's political future. In recent years, the main political parties have been the New Progressive Party and the Popular Democratic Party, with the Puerto Rican Independence Party and the Puerto Ricans for Puerto Rico Party enjoying smaller amounts of support. The first two parties favor statehood and commonwealth, respectively. The third calls for independence, and the fourth does not take a stand. In several elections in the 1990s where the status question was on the ballot, voters did not show a clear preference. During the most recent vote from November 2012, Puerto Ricans showed the strongest sign yet that they were ready for statehood.

★ **2000** BCE People from around the Orinoco River in South America are living in the region of today's Puerto Rico.

★ **1200** CE The Taino people are living in the region.

★ **1493** Christopher Columbus lands on the main island of today's Puerto Rico during his second voyage to the Americas.

★ **1508** Spanish explorer and soldier Juan Ponce de León establishes Caparra, a settlement near the site where the capital, today known as San Juan, soon develops.

★ **1513** Spain officially allows Spanish colonists to bring Africans to Puerto Rico to work as slaves.

★ **1528** French corsairs attack the town of San Germán.

★ **1625** Dutch attackers burn San Juan.

★ **1736** Coffee is introduced to Puerto Rico, and it later becomes a major export product.

★ **1873** Slavery is abolished in Puerto Rico.

★ **1898** The United States receives Puerto Rico and other territories from Spain as a result of the treaty ending the Spanish-American War.

★ **1917** The Jones Act grants U.S. citizenship to Puerto Ricans.

★ **1928** Hurricane San Felipe II kills 300 people.

★ **1947** Operation Bootstrap begins, bringing new industries to Puerto Rico.

★ **1948** Luis Muñoz Marín wins the first election for governor of Puerto Rico.

★ **1952** Puerto Rico becomes a commonwealth of the United States.

★ **1963** The Arecibo Observatory begins operation.

★ **1983** La Fortaleza in San Juan and the San Juan National Historic Site are declared a World Heritage Site by the United Nations.

★ **2003** The U.S. Navy closes its bombing-training range on the island of Vieques.

★ **2012** In a non-binding referendum on the future of Puerto Rico, pro-statehood voters won by a slight majority.

The People

When compared with most of the states in the United States, the commonwealth of Puerto Rico is small in size. However, it is densely populated. It has, on average, 1,088.2 persons living in each square mile (2.6 sq km), according to the 2010 U.S. Census. That makes it more crowded than any state except New Jersey. Approximately 3.7 million people live on the islands of Puerto Rico. Another 4.6 million people of Puerto Rican origin or descent live on the U.S. mainland. New York State, with 1.1 million, has the largest number. Florida, with 850,000, is not far behind. Other leading states are New Jersey, Pennsylvania, and Massachusetts. But no matter where they live, or where they were born, Puerto Ricans are proud of their culture and proud of the rich traditions of the Isle of Enchantment.

Criollo Culture

Puerto Rican society is diverse. Many Puerto Ricans are descendants of the native Taino people, Africans, and Spaniards. Often, their ancestry is a mix of people from these three cultures.

Quick Facts

NUYORICANS

People of Puerto Rican origin or descent who live in New York City are known as Nuyoricans. In 2010, they numbered more than 720,000, or almost 9 percent of the city's population. That total was nearly twice as large as the population of San Juan.

Colorful costumes are a part of many Puerto Rican festivals.

The people of Puerto Rico—including its street musicians—combine many different cultures and backgrounds.

Many other groups have contributed to Puerto Rican diversity, including French, Italian, and German immigrants, along with Irish and Scottish farmers, Chinese workers, and Haitian and Dominican refugees. Over the years, Puerto Ricans have blended many cultures to create one criollo culture that shapes all parts of life: language, religion, art, music, dance, food, celebrations, recreation, and more.

Language and Religion

Because it ruled the island for 400 years, Spain has had the strongest influence on Puerto Rico. Both Spanish and English are official languages, but more Puerto Ricans speak Spanish than English. Spanish is the language used in public

Santeria is practiced in Puerto Rico and many other places in the Caribbean.

schools, and English is taught as a second language. Only about 25 percent of the people speak, write, and read English fluently. However, the everyday Spanish spoken by most Puerto Ricans is often influenced by English words.

The Spaniards also introduced the Catholic religion to Puerto Rico. Today, 85 percent of the people worship as Roman Catholics. Others are of Protestant or Jewish faith. However, many people follow a religion known as Santeria, a blend of African, Taino, and Catholic spiritual beliefs and practices.

The Arts

Through the centuries, Puerto Rico's unique culture has inspired local artists to create remarkable paintings (including murals), craft items, and sculptures. The earliest well-known artist was an eighteenth-century painter named José Campeche, the son of a freed slave and an immigrant from the Canary Islands (off the northwest coast of Africa). Campeche painted religious scenes and portraits, as did the European artists of his time.

Many craft traditions have roots in the cultures of Puerto Ricans' ancestors. Skills for these crafts have been passed from one generation to the next. Since

Vejigante masks are supposed to make the wearer look like a fearsome evil spirit.

the sixteenth century, whole families of artisans have carved wooden statues called santos. In Latin America, santos are figures typically showing Catholic saints. African and Taino craftspeople in Puerto Rico also carved statues of their gods. The artisans of each Puerto Rican culture influenced one another, creating this unique art form.

A distinctively Puerto Rican tradition is the masked *vejigante* character seen at many festivals. Vejigantes represent evil spirits from an old Spanish legend. Puerto Ricans created this character by combining the idea of evil spirits with African mask-making skills and the Spanish tradition of wearing costumes in carnival celebrations. The masks have brightly painted horns, snouts, and devilish expressions.

A type of lace called *mundillo* is another Puerto Rican handmade item. Only artisans in Spain and Puerto Rico know how to make it. The traditional center of mundillo is the town of Moca, which has a museum devoted to this rare, 500-year-old craft. Nearby Isabela holds a weaving festival each spring that celebrates mundillo.

Music is another favorite art form in Puerto Rico. "Everything that happens in Puerto Rico is accompanied by music," says one Puerto Rican.

Puerto Rican musical styles are an exotic blend of Taino, African, and Spanish rhythms and instruments. The Tainos danced to story-songs in ceremonial dances called *areytos*. They played instruments such as maracas, which are dried gourds filled with beans that rattle when shaken, and guiros, which are notched gourds that are scraped with a stick. Africans brought drums to Puerto Rico, and the Spanish brought guitars.

Puerto Ricans combined all of these influences to create unique musical sounds and dances such as *lamentos*, which are sad ballads, *danzas*, which are like ballroom dances with a Caribbean beat, and the *bomba* and *plena*, which are dances with African roots. In the bomba, drummers and dancers challenge each other. The plena is usually performed to instruments such as drums and tambourines, along with a guitar and a guiro or maraca.

Modern music in Puerto Rico also includes the lively and rhythmic merengue, salsa, reggaeton, and Latin pop and jazz. Many Puerto Rican musicians have become famous around the world. Examples include the native Puerto Ricans José Feliciano and Ricky Martin, along with the New York–born Tito Puente, Marc Anthony, and Jennifer Lopez.

Classical music in Puerto Rico owes much to the great cello player Pablo Casals. Born in Spain to a Puerto Rican mother, he spent most of his final years in Puerto Rico, where he died in 1973. The world-renowned Casals Festival, held in San Juan every year, was founded by him in 1956. He established the Puerto Rico Symphony Orchestra in 1958 and the Conservatory of Music of Puerto Rico in 1959.

Highly popular today, the bomba originated in Puerto Rico in the seventeenth century.

MAKING A VEJIGANTE MASK

Historians believe Tainos, Africans, and Spaniards who settled Puerto Rico's islands made masks for their festivals. The tradition continues today.

WHAT YOU NEED

5 or 6 sheets of newspaper

Ruler with a metal edge

Plastic wrap

Large mixing bowl

1 balloon large enough to blow up to the size of your head

1 bottle of white glue (4-ounce [118-milliliter] size)

Small bucket (or large plastic tub)

Water

Stirring stick

Styrofoam "peanuts," cut-up egg cartons, sponges, cardboard, or foil

Masking tape or double-sided clear tape

Acrylic paints in various colors

Paintbrushes

Scissors

String or a rubber band about 1 foot (30 cm) long

Spread two to three layers of newspaper over a work area. From the remaining newspaper sheets, tear several dozen strips approximately 1 inch (2.5 cm) wide and 8 to 9 inches (20 to 23 cm) long. Tearing against the ruler's metal edge makes the job easy. Torn strips stick better than cut ones do. Lay a sheet of plastic wrap across the top of the mixing bowl so that several inches hang down to catch drips. Blow up the balloon and rest it on the plastic wrap over the mixing bowl.

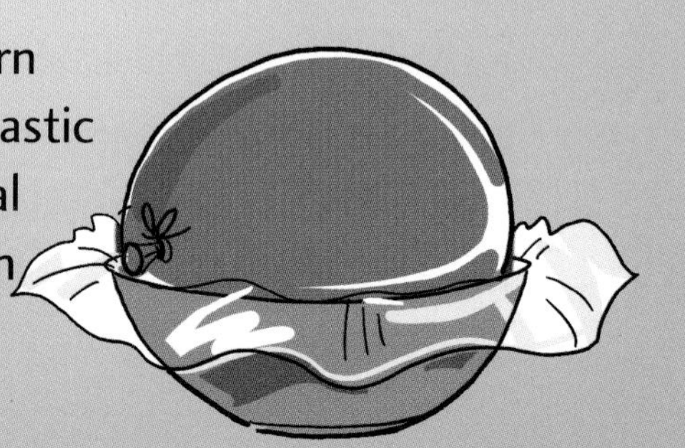

Pour the entire bottle of glue into the bucket. Fill the empty glue bottle twice with cold water—2 bottles of water to 1 bottle of glue—each time pouring and stirring the water into the glue with the stirring stick. The mixture should be very runny.

One by one, dip each newspaper strip into the glue mixture. Let any extra glue drip back into the bucket. Apply the strips to the "face-up" side of the balloon so that the edges overlap. Allow the strips to dry completely for several hours. After the first layer is dry, apply another layer of newspaper strips over the first and allow them to dry for several hours again or overnight.

Use the cardboard, egg cartons, Styrofoam, foil, or sponges to make facial features like horns, a nose, or bulging eyeballs. Tape down the features with the masking tape or clear tape.

Paint your mask and allow it to dry completely. Pop the balloon, and gently pull it away from the mask.

You can trim away any shreds or uneven edges with the scissors. Carefully make a hole on each side of the mask. Tie the string or rubber band to one side of the mask, then to the other.

Your mask is ready to wear.

Thousands of people fill Calle San Sebastián in San Juan for its annual street festival.

Festivities

Festivals and celebrations are frequent in Puerto Rico. They vary in custom, but they typically feature live music, dance, costumes, crafts, parades, and traditional foods. Many types of festivals celebrate harvests of crops such as sugarcane, flowers, coffee beans, and pineapples. Major music festivals include the Casals Festival, the Puerto Rico JazzFest, and the National Bomba and Plena Fiesta. Political, religious, and ethnic festivals are held throughout the year. Puerto Ricans, being citizens of the United States, honor all U.S. holidays, as well as their own national holidays. Some of these national holidays are Abolition of Slavery Day (March 22), the birthday of Luis Muñoz Rivera (third Monday in July), Puerto Rican Constitution Day (July 25), and Discovery of Puerto Rico Day (November 19).

Each of the seventy-eight municipios, or municipalities, holds a festival honoring the town's patron saint. Fiestas patronales, as they are called, commonly begin with a church service on a Friday, two to twelve days before the saint's official holiday. After the religious events end, everyone leaves the church and goes out into the town plaza. Then, for as long as two weeks, musicians play day and night. Food vendors, farmers, and artisans line the plaza, and people dance, shop, and join in parades. Some of the largest and most popular of the saints' festivals are Festival of Saint James (Fiesta de Santiago Apóstol) and Festival of Saint John the Baptist (Fiesta de San Juan Bautista). Other important religious celebrations are Easter week (Semana Santa, or Holy Week) and the Christmas season (Las Navidades). During these holidays, many city dwellers go back to the countryside, where their families, including grandparents, cousins, aunts, and uncles, gather to celebrate.

Food and Fun

While typical U.S. foods can be found in markets and restaurants, Puerto Rico also has its own cuisine, or style of cooking. Food is a major part of every celebration and event. Farmers' markets, outdoor food stalls, and open-air cafés all send their tempting aromas into the streets. Fresh fruits such as pineapples, mangoes, coconuts, papayas, and avocados are plentiful.

The word *barbecue* comes from a Taino word. For hundreds of years, Puerto Ricans have cooked meats such as chicken and pork on outdoor barbecues. Rice and pigeon peas (similar to sweet peas) are included in a meal almost every day in most households. Plantains are another favorite food. They look similar to bananas, but plantains taste more like sweet potatoes. Cooks prepare plantains by frying, boiling, or sometimes mashing them. Cooks use a variety of sauces to flavor many meats and vegetables. One example is *sofrito*, which is made from peppers, onions, garlic, tomatoes, and spices, commonly along with bacon or ham.

Puerto Rican markets feature a wide variety of fresh fruits.

RECIPE FOR A TROPICAL FRUIT SMOOTHIE

Puerto Ricans make a variety of drinks with coconut, mango, pineapple, banana, or papaya. On market day, it is fun to stop and sip a cool *batida* (smoothie), or make your own.

WHAT YOU NEED

1 banana

1 ripe mango (if unavailable, use either a peach, $\frac{1}{2}$ cup [125 ml] pineapple slices, or $\frac{1}{2}$ cup papaya)

$\frac{1}{4}$ cup (60 ml) orange or pineapple juice

$\frac{1}{4}$ cup (60 ml) milk

6 ice cubes

1 tablespoon (15 ml) honey

1 teaspoon (5 ml) vanilla

Peel the banana and slice it into approximately 2-inch (5-cm) slices. Set aside. With an adult's help, peel the mango with a paring knife. Slice off 2-inch (5-cm) chunks of fruit and set aside.

Measure the juice and the milk, and pour the liquids into a blender. Add the fruit slices. Place the blender lid on tightly. Process the mixture at high speed for about 30 seconds.

Add an ice cube and process for another 30 seconds. Repeat for each ice cube. Add the honey and vanilla. Replace the lid and process for another 5 to 10 seconds. Pour the drink into two glasses. Make a toast. Your batida will be thick, frothy, healthful, and delicious.

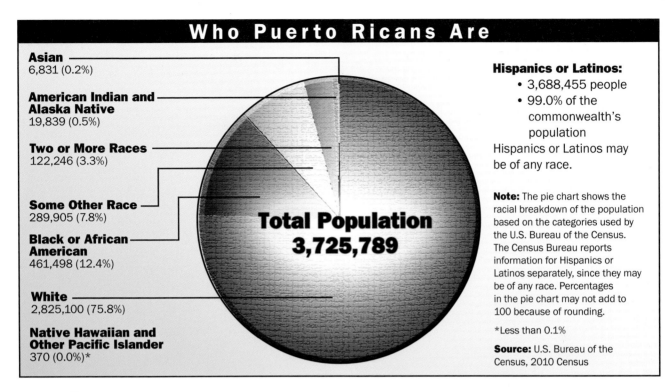

Who Puerto Ricans Are

Asian
6,831 (0.2%)

American Indian and Alaska Native
19,839 (0.5%)

Two or More Races
122,246 (3.3%)

Some Other Race
289,905 (7.8%)

Black or African American
461,498 (12.4%)

White
2,825,100 (75.8%)

Native Hawaiian and Other Pacific Islander
370 (0.0%)*

Total Population 3,725,789

Hispanics or Latinos:
- 3,688,455 people
- 99.0% of the commonwealth's population

Hispanics or Latinos may be of any race.

Note: The pie chart shows the racial breakdown of the population based on the categories used by the U.S. Bureau of the Census. The Census Bureau reports information for Hispanics or Latinos separately, since they may be of any race. Percentages in the pie chart may not add to 100 because of rounding.

*Less than 0.1%

Source: U.S. Bureau of the Census, 2010 Census

Sports

Puerto Rico's mild climate is good for many outdoor activities. Puerto Ricans enjoy boating, fishing, swimming, surfing, hiking, tennis, and golf year-round. In plazas everywhere, people can be seen seated at tables in the shade, playing serious games of dominoes or chess. Other sports passions are baseball and boxing. The Tainos enjoyed ball games centuries ago, and today Puerto Ricans play baseball year-round. Many Major League players from the United States play winter baseball in Puerto Rico. Also, hundreds of talented Major League players have come from Puerto Rico or are of Puerto Rican ancestry. Among those born in Puerto Rico are

Surfers can ride the waves year-round in Puerto Rico's warm waters.

Today, more than one out of every ten Puerto Ricans lives within the city of San Juan.

Roberto Clemente, Orlando Cepeda, Juan González, Javy López, Sandy Alomar, Bernie Williams, José Cruz, Carlos Delgado, Jorge Posada, Iván Rodríguez, and Carlos Beltrán.

City and Countryside

During Operation Bootstrap, people began leaving their homes in the countryside (called *el campo* in Spanish) to move to jobs in the cities. Today, the cities are crowded.

Suburban sprawl, made up of endless rows of concrete houses, spreads outside the cities. People worry that Puerto Rico is becoming dangerously overcrowded. The crowding can cause serious problems, such as a shortage of jobs, rising crime rates, and a higher cost of living.

However, others are hopeful. "It used to be," says a former San Juan business owner, "that anyone with an education, or anyone who wanted an education, went to the United States and didn't come back." But more recently, at times when economic opportunities seemed more promising in Puerto Rico, many of those islanders who migrated have returned.

Although today only a small percentage of the Puerto Rican population lives in the countryside, people remain loyal to the small towns and villages many of them came from. During major holidays, families return to their hometowns. Many mountain villages look much the same as they did a century or more ago. Throughout the countryside, town plazas are lively centers of action. Some city dwellers are rethinking their move away from the country. They want to end their dependence on factory jobs and return to farming. During summer's heat, many Puerto Ricans escape to the mountains to relax.

Whether from the city or countryside, Puerto Ricans love their land. They treasure its rich culture and are proud of its unique place in the world.

Francisco Oller: Artist

Born in 1833 in the town of Bayamón, Francisco Manuel Oller y Cestero was the first important Puerto Rican artist to study in Europe. He returned to his homeland to teach and to paint. Oller took part in the development of the style of painting called impressionism. He painted Puerto Rico's natural beauty as well as its social problems. His paintings are displayed in museums around the world. Some show landscapes. Many portray aspects of island life, from portraits of governors, to scenes of slaves working on sugar plantations, to paintings illustrating everyday activities.

Lola Rodríguez de Tió: Poet

Lola Rodríguez de Tió was born in San Germán in 1843. She was a descendant of Puerto Rico's first governor, Juan Ponce de León. Rodríguez de Tió became known throughout Latin America for her political poetry. She championed women's rights, abolition of slavery, and independence for Puerto Rico. Throughout Puerto Rico, schools, other buildings, and streets are named in her honor.

Roberto Clemente: Baseball Player

Roberto Clemente was born in Carolina, Puerto Rico, in 1934. He was the first Latin American inducted into the Baseball Hall of Fame. An outfielder for the Pittsburgh Pirates with a career batting average of .317, he was named the National League's Most Valuable Player in 1966 and the World Series MVP in 1971. At the age of 38, while on a mission bringing supplies to earthquake victims in Nicaragua, he was killed in a plane crash. The Roberto Clemente Award is presented every year to a Major League Baseball player who combines outstanding skills on the field with charitable work.

Sila Calderón: Politician

Born in 1942 in San Juan, Sila María Calderón earned a bachelor's degree in government at Manhattanville College in Purchase, New York, and also studied public administration at the University of Puerto Rico. A member of the Popular Democratic Party, she was the first woman to be elected governor of Puerto Rico, holding that office from 2001 to 2005. Before that, she served in such government posts as secretary of state of Puerto Rico and mayor of San Juan. She has also had a successful career as a businesswoman.

Antonia Novello: Physician

Antonia Novello was born in Fajardo in 1944. She received her medical degree from the University of Puerto Rico in 1970. She joined the U.S. Public Health Service in 1978 and began working for the National Institutes of Health. In 1990, she was appointed by President George H. W. Bush to the post of surgeon general of the United States. She was the first woman and the first Hispanic to hold that office.

Ricky Martin: Singer and Actor

Enrique Martin Morales, who uses the stage name Ricky Martin, was born in San Juan in 1971. He began appearing in TV commercials at age six. In 1984, he joined the Latino pop group Menudo, remaining with the group for five years. Later, Martin became a leading man in Broadway theater and a Grammy-winning pop star, best known for the 1999 hit song "Livin' La Vida Loca."

one of Puerto Rico's biggest festivals. The celebration honors Saint Sebastian, whose official day is January 20. The event attracts huge numbers of people with music, dancing, performers, food, a parade, and displays of arts and crafts.

★ Carnival

The city of Ponce, on the south coast, is famous for its colorful Carnival, or Mardi Gras, occurring the week before Lent begins. Lent is a forty-day period of fasting before the Christian holiday of Easter. The Carnival celebration features a parade, vejigantes, and an abundance of music, dancing, and food.

★ Three Kings' Day

January 6, Three Kings' Day, marks the end of the Christmas season, or Las Navidades. On the eve of Three Kings' Day, children put shoe boxes filled with grass under their beds. According to legend, three kings riding camels visit each house on that night. After the camels eat the grass, the kings fill the shoe boxes with gifts. The next morning, January 6, children awaken to holiday presents and treats.

★ San Juan Bautista Day

San Juan Bautista is Spanish for Saint John the Baptist. June 24 is that saint's day, celebrated with food, music, and good times—beginning at the stroke of midnight, when people jump into the ocean backward, a tradition meant to renew good luck in the year ahead. The partying takes place not only in San Juan but also elsewhere in Puerto Rico.

★ Calle San Sebastián Festival

In mid-January, Calle San Sebastián, or Saint Sebastian Street, in the old section of San Juan is the center of

★ Aibonito Flower Festival

For more than a week in late June and early July, the mountain town of Aibonito comes alive with Puerto Rico's biggest festival devoted to plants and flowers. Fields of roses, lilies, orchids, and other flowers burst forth with color and aroma in the town's Festival de las Flores. Thousands of visitors come to buy flowers and enjoy crafts, music, dance, and traditional foods.

★ Fiesta de Santiago Apóstol

Santiago Apóstol is Spanish for Saint James, whose holiday is July 25. James is the patron saint of several towns. But the one with the most famous celebration is Loíza, a town not far from San Juan. Over several days, people pay homage with parades, Afro–Puerto Rican music and dance, traditional foods, and spectacular vejigantes.

★ Hatillo Masks Festival

On December 28, the northwestern town of Hatillo holds the third (after Ponce and Loíza) of Puerto Rico's major annual festivals involving masks. It reenacts the biblical story of King Herod, who ordered all baby boys to be killed in hopes of doing away with the baby Jesus. Masked devil-soldiers in colorful costumes run through the streets of Hatillo, looking for children. But it is just a game, and as in all Puerto Rican festivals, there is lively music, dancing, and traditional foods.

How the Government Works

Puerto Rico underwent centuries of changing rules and governments before it became a commonwealth of the United States in 1952. Perhaps that status will change again. Meanwhile, people in Puerto Rico live under three levels of government: local, commonwealth, and federal.

Levels of Government

Residents of U.S. states commonly live under more than one level of local government, such as city and county. Puerto Rico, however, has only one level. The commonwealth is divided into seventy-eight municipios. Each municipio elects a mayor and an assembly for a four-year term of office (and there is no limit on the number of terms an official can serve). A municipio with many residents, equivalent to a big city, typically has a larger assembly than a less populated municipio, which might be compared to a town or village on the U.S. mainland.

> ### *In Their Own Words*
>
> *The dignity of the human being is inviolable. All men are equal before the law. No discrimination shall be made on account of race, color, sex, birth, social origin or condition, or political or religious ideas.*
>
> —Constitution of Puerto Rico

La Fortaleza, the governor's residence, overlooks San Juan Bay.

HISTORIC MANSION

The governor's official residence, called La Fortaleza, was originally built in 1530–1540 as a fortress to guard the entrance to San Juan's harbor. It is the oldest continuously used executive mansion in the New World. Together with the forts in the San Juan National Historic Site, La Fortaleza has been recognized by the United Nations as a World Heritage Site.

The second level of government in Puerto Rico is the commonwealth government. In March 1952, the people were asked to approve a constitution that had been drawn up by their representatives subject to approval by Congress. More than 80 percent of the people voted in favor of the document, and Congress approved it a few months later. Many of the provisions found in the constitution are similar to those found in U.S. state constitutions and the federal Constitution. For example, there is a bill of rights, and there are three branches of government—the executive branch, the legislative (law-making) branch, and the judicial branch (the courts). In the commonwealth, the executive branch is headed by a governor, who is elected by the voters. The governor, in turn, has the important role of appointing judges and other executive officeholders. Citizens also elect the members of the law-making body, known as the legislative assembly. It consists of two chambers: a senate and a house of representatives. The commonwealth has its own flag and its own official anthem, or song.

Puerto Rico relies on the U.S. federal government to provide many functions that it also carries out for the fifty states, such as postal service, oversight of communications systems, military defense, customs and immigration enforcement, and the conducting of foreign relations. Puerto Rico belongs to the federal court system of the United States and is under the jurisdiction of the U.S. First Circuit Court of Appeals. Puerto Ricans are U.S. citizens and are free to come and go to the mainland of the United States without having to get a visa, or special permission, which is often required when a person travels abroad.

Branches of Government

EXECUTIVE ★ ★ ★ ★ ★ ★ ★ ★

The governor is the powerful head of the executive branch. The governor appoints all judges and all department heads, subject to approval by the senate. He or she signs bills into law and can also refuse to sign bills. This refusal is called a veto. The governor is elected to a four-year term, and there is no limit to how many times he or she can be reelected.

LEGISLATIVE ★ ★ ★ ★ ★ ★ ★ ★

As of 2012, the legislative assembly is usually made up of twenty-seven senators and fifty-one members of the house of representatives. Most members of the legislative assembly represent a particular area, or district. For the senate, Puerto Rico is divided into eight districts, each of which elects two senators. For the house of representatives, Puerto Rico is divided into forty districts, with each electing one representative. In addition, eleven senators and eleven members of the house of representatives are elected "at large"—that is, they represent Puerto Rico as a whole.

All members of the legislative assembly are elected to four-year terms, with no limit on the number of terms. If voters elect members from one political party to hold more than two-thirds of the seats in either the house or the senate, then extra seats are added to that chamber and assigned to members of the minority parties on an at-large basis.

The government asked voters to decide, in the November 2012 election, whether they wanted to reduce the number of members in the legislative assembly, which some people considered too large and expensive.

JUDICIAL ★ ★ ★ ★ ★ ★ ★ ★

The judicial branch is a system of courts made up of the supreme court, court of appeals, and the court of first instance. The governor appoints all judges, with approval of the senate. The highest court, the supreme court, is made up of nine justices, who serve until the age of seventy. The supreme court hears appeals of decisions made by lower courts and decides whether laws are in accordance with the commonwealth constitution. It also oversees the court system. The court of appeals, whose judges serve sixteen-year terms, hears challenges to rulings made in lower courts. Judges in the court of first instance are appointed to twelve-year terms. This court is divided into two sections: superior court and municipal court. Superior courts hear the major civil and criminal trial cases. Municipal courts make decisions on small claims and lesser crimes.

REPRESENTATION IN THE GLOBAL ARENA

Unlike the U.S. states, Puerto Rico has its own Olympic teams and also competes as a separate nation in other international competitions in such sports as baseball, basketball, boxing, diving, soccer, and track and field. It is an associate member of such groups as the World Health Organization, the United Nations Economic Commission for Latin America and the Caribbean, and the World Tourism Organization.

When living in Puerto Rico, Puerto Ricans do not pay U.S. federal income tax. However, they do pay federal Social Security tax. They can collect Social Security benefits and some other types of income payments from the U.S. government. (Social Security benefits help people who are retired or unable to work.) Puerto Ricans can enlist in the military of the United States and are included in the military draft, when it is

Puerto Rico's legislative assembly meets in the Capitol in San Juan.

in effect. Citizens in Puerto Rico can vote in the presidential primary elections of the two major political parties in the United States, the Democrats and the Republicans. But they cannot vote in the main presidential election. They do elect one representative to the U.S. House of Representatives, who serves a four-year term. However, that representative—the resident commissioner—is not allowed to vote on legislation.

The Status Question

Puerto Ricans have been debating one major political issue for a long time. Do they want Puerto Rico to be a U.S. state? Do they want it to remain a commonwealth? Or do they want it to be a truly independent country? Everyone has an opinion.

In 1967, 1991, 1993, 1998, and 2012, voters attempted to resolve this issue. But the issue is a complicated one. Each of the three main political parties in Puerto Rico in those years had—and still has today—a different point of view. The New Progressive Party, for example, says that Puerto Rico should become the fifty-first state. Supporters of statehood want their votes to count on matters affecting the United States. If Puerto Rico were to become the fifty-first state, then citizens would be able to vote for the U.S. president, two U.S. senators, and members of the U.S. House of Representatives with full voting rights. Also, with statehood, Puerto Rico would receive additional funds from the federal government.

On the other hand, the Puerto Rican Independence Party says that Puerto Rico has been no more than a colony and should now become an independent nation. Followers of the party believe that a new constitution, one that Puerto Ricans write independently of the United States, would better protect their Hispanic language and culture. They point out that if Puerto Rico were to become independent, it would be able to manage its own money, its radio and television broadcasts, its immigration laws, its trade with other countries, and most importantly, its own defense. Some Puerto Ricans dislike the U.S. military's controlling their land, waters, and air space.

The Popular Democratic Party, however, wants to continue commonwealth status. Commonwealth supporters believe that the tax benefits, trade partnership, and protection of the U.S. military, as well as citizenship rights, offer the best of both worlds. Puerto Ricans are, on average, wealthier and better educated than most of their Caribbean neighbors. This prosperity, says the Popular Democratic Party, is due to the commonwealth association with the United States.

In the 1967 election, a majority—60 percent—voted to keep the status of commonwealth, 39 percent were for statehood, and only about 1 percent wanted independence. But the results of later elections were not so clear. In 1991, Puerto Ricans were asked whether they wanted to approve a constitutional amendment that would, among other things, assert the right to freely decide between the three alternatives. "No" received 53 percent of the votes. In 1993, 48.6 percent voted for commonwealth status, 46.3 percent for statehood, and 4.4 percent for independence. The governor in 1993 belonged to the pro-statehood New Progressive Party.

Hoping to get a better result, he and his supporters in 1998 presented voters with a ballot that had five choices: statehood, "territorial" commonwealth, "free association" (roughly midway between commonwealth and independence), independence, and "none of the above." Statehood received 46.5 percent, and independence 2.5 percent. Free association was the choice of 0.3 percent and commonwealth was chosen by 0.1 percent. The biggest vote share, 50.3 percent, went to "none of the above."

In 2012, with the New Progressive Party once again in control of the governor's office, Governor Luis Fortuño and the legislative assembly scheduled a new vote on the status question. Although for the first time a slim majority of Puerto Ricans voted in favor of statehood, voters also elected a new governor, Alejandro Garcia Padilla of the pro-commonwealth Popular Democratic Party. The debate continues.

Supporters of Puerto Rico's becoming a separate nation take part in a Puerto Rican Independence Party march in Guánica.

How a Bill Becomes a Law

Like the United States and most of its fifty state governments, Puerto Rico has two chambers in its legislative assembly: a senate and a house of representatives. Each of these chambers is sometimes referred to as a house. The chief duty of their members, also called legislators, is to create laws. A legislator in either of the two houses can introduce a proposed law, which is called a bill. One exception, however, is that all tax-related laws must begin in the house of representatives. When a legislator has an idea for a bill, the bill must be printed and given to a committee to decide whether it is a good idea.

Each committee within a house focuses on a particular topic, such as education, agriculture, natural resources, health, transportation, or taxes. During committee meetings, members discuss the bill and listen to people who have come to express their views about it. If a committee approves a bill, it is

The artworks on the inside of the Capitol dome show scenes from Puerto Rico's history.

presented to all the members of the house. The other legislators debate the bill and may suggest changes, or amendments. The bill is then put to a vote within the house where it was created. If the bill receives a majority of the votes, it is sent to the other house. When the bill is received in the other house, it goes through much the same process of committee discussion and voting. If the second house wants to amend the bill, the two houses must come to an agreement on the final wording for the bill to be sent on to the governor for his or her consideration.

If the bill does pass in both houses, it is presented to the governor. The governor can sign the bill, making it law. Or the governor can refuse to sign the bill and return it to the house where it began, sending along with the bill his or her objections or suggestions for changes. This action is called a veto. If the bill is vetoed, it will still become law if the two houses decide to reconsider it and two-thirds of the members of each house then vote in favor of it.

When the governor wants to veto a bill, he or she usually must return it to the legislature within ten days. Otherwise, the bill will become law without the governor's signature. If the legislature is no longer in session, however, the governor does not have to return a bill in order to veto it.

Contacting Lawmakers

★ ★ ★ ★ ★ ★ ★ ★ ★ ★ ★

The websites for the two chambers of the legislative assembly tell how to contact lawmakers. The sites are in Spanish. For the senate, go to

http://www.senadopr.us

and find "Senadores" near the top of the page. The menu that drops down lists different groups of senators (majority, minority, at large, and individual districts). Clicking on one of the groups will take you to a page listing party affiliation, telephone number, and address for each senator in the group.

For the house of representatives, go to

http://www.camaraderepresentantes.org

and click on "Representantes" near the top of the page. This will take you to a page with pictures of all the representatives. To get information on a particular one, click on his or her picture.

Making a Living

The Tainos grew a healthful variety of crops and had plenty of food to meet their needs. When the Spanish colonized Puerto Rico and took over most of the farmland, they planted just a few moneymaking crops to trade with Europe. Among the first plantation crops were sugarcane and, later, coffee. Farmers grew sugarcane in the valleys, and they planted coffee beans in the mountains.

As one citizen recounts, "Puerto Rico grows the finest coffee in the world. All the houses of kings once ordered coffee from the island growers. Every year, the best of the crop was delivered to the pope." The United States was also an important importer. At the height of Puerto Rico's success as a coffee exporter, a couple of severe hurricanes at the end of the nineteenth century destroyed the big plantations. It took years for the farms to recover. When they did, the United States had begun buying coffee from Brazil. Because of this, the coffee plantations declined. Hurricane Georges in 1998 had a devastating effect on coffee production, but coffee farmers are working at growing coffee again.

The United States continued to import huge quantities of sugarcane until the 1940s, after which sugarcane production dropped. Only a few plantations remain today, as a result of competition from sugar-beet farming in the United States and around the world.

In the second half of the twentieth century, manufacturing medications became a major industry in Puerto Rico.

Workers & Industries

Industry	Number of People Working in That Industry	Percentage of All Workers Who Are Working in That Industry
Education and health care	251,121	22.4%
Wholesale and retail businesses	184,505	16.4%
Government	120,709	10.7%
Publishing, media, entertainment, hotels, and restaurants	110,759	9.9%
Professionals, scientists, and managers	106,888	9.5%
Manufacturing	106,361	9.5%
Construction	65,742	5.9%
Other services	63,402	5.6%
Banking and finance, insurance, and real estate	58,424	5.2%
Transportation and public utilities	42,777	3.8%
Farming, fishing, forestry, and mining	12,562	1.1%
Totals	**1,123,250**	**100%**

Notes: Figures above do not include people in the armed forces.
"Professionals" includes people such as doctors and lawyers.

Source: U.S. Bureau of the Census, 2010 estimates

Currently, only about 1 percent of workers in Puerto Rico are involved in farming. But many people feel the need to develop more farms. They are worried that Puerto Rico relies too heavily on the United States for food. Rice, for example, is very important in all Puerto Rican kitchens. The nearby Dominican Republic produces huge amounts of rice, yet Puerto Rico grows very little. Instead, it imports tons of the grain from the United States and other countries each year.

Puerto Rican farmers, especially in the western region, grow such crops as fruits and native root vegetables. Citizens can buy fresh homegrown foods at weekly farmers' markets held in the central plazas of cities and towns. The mainstay of Puerto Rican agriculture—the chief source of income—is dairy and livestock farming, such as the production of milk, eggs, and meat from cows and chickens. Leading crops in terms of market value are plantains, coffee, and ornamental plants. The chief agricultural product exported by Puerto Rico is rum. It is usually made, however, from molasses that is imported.

Young coffee trees may be first grown in pots, before they are planted in the ground.

Natural Resources

Puerto Rico is a small island group with limited natural resources. Many of its forests have been cut to make way for plantations and housing. Today, few trees are left to harvest for lumber. Some forests, however, are being replanted.

Fishing was once a very typical way to earn a living. But it is no longer a major source of income. Many people who fish commercially also hold other jobs. In addition to fish, the seafood catch includes lobsters, shrimp, crabs, and conchs. Fish farming is carried out on a small scale, mainly involving the raising of tilapia, shrimp, and ornamental fish in fish ponds.

Valuable metals such as gold, copper, iron, and silver were once mined in Puerto Rico, but the mines have closed. Today, the chief minerals produced are sand, gravel, lime, clay, and stone—used to build houses, roads, and the like— along with salt.

Transportation

"It used to take half a day to get to Mayagüez. Now, there are highways everywhere, and it takes twenty minutes," comments a man from San Germán.

Quick Facts

SUPER TELESCOPE

Located amid the mountains of northwest Puerto Rico, the Arecibo Observatory is the site of the world's largest single-dish radio telescope. The dish is 1,000 feet (305 m) wide and covers about 20 acres (8 ha). There, astronomers and other scientists from around the world study remote celestial objects such as the pulsating stars called pulsars, as well as relatively close-by objects in our own solar system.

The Tren Urbano has sixteen stations along its 10.7-mile (17.2-km) line.

In the past two decades, roads and highways have been extensively improved. There are nearly 17,000 miles (27,000 km) of roads and more than 2.4 million cars. Streets are often packed with the despised *tapones*, or traffic jams.

"Oh," says one shopkeeper, "you should see the cars thread their way through Old San Juan. They go one after the other all day and on into the night!" To help relieve some of the congestion, a mass transportation system, called the Tren Urbano, or Urban Train, opened in the San Juan area at the end of 2004. The line was the first rapid transit system in the Caribbean.

While cars, buses, and the Tren Urbano move people around Puerto Rico, airplanes and boats move people to and from the commonwealth. San Juan has a large international airport, named after Luis Muñoz Marín. There also are at least ten smaller public airports in Puerto Rico. Planes and ferry boats serve the islands of Culebra and Vieques. San Juan and Ponce are among the Caribbean's chief ports for container ships and cruise ships. In fact, San Juan is the biggest and busiest port for cruise ships in the Caribbean.

Manufacturing

Almost 10 percent of the labor force in Puerto Rico is employed in manufacturing. In the late 1940s, people began leaving their traditional fishing and farming jobs to go to the cities to work in the new factories launched by Operation Bootstrap. The U.S. government encouraged industrial development in

Operation Bootstrap by giving companies from the United States and other countries special tax breaks, loans, and research help if they would set up factories in Puerto Rico. Many large corporations are there to this day, including General Electric, Hewlett-Packard, Johnson & Johnson, Pfizer, and Procter & Gamble. Puerto Rican factories make clothing, medicines, chemicals, electronics, and many other useful products.

Over the years, laws concerning taxes and related matters changed in the United States and a number of other countries, making Puerto Rico a less beneficial place to do business. As a result, many companies reduced the number of employees they hired in Puerto Rico and moved factories to countries where labor was cheaper. Yet, Puerto Rico still has an educated workforce, so jobs involving high-technology, chemical, and medical products remain an important part of the economy. Some of the most commonly prescribed medicines in the United States are manufactured in Puerto Rico.

Service Jobs

Most members of Puerto Rico's labor force are employed in service jobs. These jobs include all types of work not involved in making actual things—not involved, that is, in such activities as growing crops or manufacturing products. Service workers include, for example, hotel clerks, restaurant workers, health care workers, lawyers, shopkeepers, and bankers. They also include people who work for the government, such as officials, public school teachers, police officers, and firefighters.

Many service jobs lie in Puerto Rico's large tourism industry. Each year, roughly 5 million visitors come to Puerto Rico, 3 million of them from the United States. Although the tourists' money is welcome, some Puerto Ricans believe the many hotels, restaurants, and cruise ships add to crowding on the islands and strain resources.

One form of tourism that protects the environment while still providing jobs is eco-tourism. Eco-tourists are people who enjoy visiting a place and studying its natural areas. They stay in small inns or in people's houses and eat at local restaurants. Eco-tourists come to Puerto Rico to kayak in the lagoons, hike in the rain forest, bird-watch, spelunk in caves, snorkel at coral reefs, and study other natural features. The Puerto Rican eco-tourism industry is working with scientists, environmentalists, local businesspeople, government officials, and others to preserve and protect the commonwealth's tropical beauty. Possessing such a special place in the world, Puerto Ricans have a bounty that they are proud to share.

The tourism industry provides jobs for tour guides and many other types of workers.

Coffee

In the 1800s, Puerto Rico coffee plantations were among the most important in the world. Coffee growing slumped for many decades in the twentieth century, but it is still carried on. Today's farmers typically grow their coffee high in the mountains, often at 2,500 to 2,800 feet (760 to 850 m) above sea level or even higher. Their coffee has a fine aroma and a medium bittersweetness and is prized by gourmet coffee drinkers.

Medications

In recent years, some of Puerto Rico's pharmaceutical manufacturing facilities have moved elsewhere, but many remain. As of 2011, at least a dozen major companies were in Puerto Rico, and they had some 30 manufacturing operations. The industry employs about 20 percent of Puerto Rico's manufacturing workforce and produces many of the top-selling drugs in the United States. Among the pharmaceutical companies operating in Puerto Rico are Eli Lilly, Johnson & Johnson, Merck, and Pfizer.

Salt Mining

The oldest industry in Puerto Rico is salt mining. The largest salt extraction operation is at Cabo Rojo on the southwest coast. The area is said to have served as a source of salt since the time of the Tainos.

Tourism

Approximately 5 million people visit Puerto Rico each year and spend some $3.5 billion there. Many arrive via cruise ship. Others come by plane. Luxury hotels, year-round warm weather, and sandy beaches are major attractions.

Textiles

Fine needlework such as lace-making is a centuries-old skill among Puerto Rican women. The craft became popular in the United States, too, when influential Americans such as the wife of inventor Thomas Edison and President Franklin Delano Roosevelt and his wife, Eleanor, purchased traditional Puerto Rican textiles. Later, clothing manufacturers from the United States set up factories. Today, clothing manufacture is a leading industry, and the craft of lace-making remains popular.

Puerto Rican Santos

Since the sixteenth century, Puerto Rican artists have carved santos—wooden figures of Catholic saints—for display in people's homes. For many years, there were few priests in Puerto Rico, so people often worshiped at home altars or family chapels decorated with santos. Modern carvers continue the tradition. Art collectors, folk-art museums, and galleries around the world feature antique and modern Puerto Rican santos in their collections.

The flag of the commonwealth is based on a design created at the end of the nineteenth century. It resembles the Cuban flag, with the colors reversed. There are five stripes: three red and two white. The red stripes signify the blood that feeds the three branches of the commonwealth's government. The white stripes represent freedom and the rights of citizens. A white star inside a blue triangle stands for the commonwealth. The triangle represents the three branches of the government. The flag was officially adopted in 1952.

In the sixteenth century, the king of Spain presented a seal to Puerto Rico. Figures from that seal are part of the island's present seal. A lamb represents peace and brotherhood. The letters F and I stand for Ferdinand and Isabella, the king and queen of Spain in the late 1400s and early 1500s. Old symbols associated with Spain, such as the Towers of Castile, the Lions of Leon, the crosses of Jerusalem, and various Spanish flags also appear. The motto Joannes Est Nomen Ejus *is Latin for "John Is His Name." It refers to Saint John, or San Juan Bautista, after whom Puerto Rico was originally named.*

PUERTO RICO

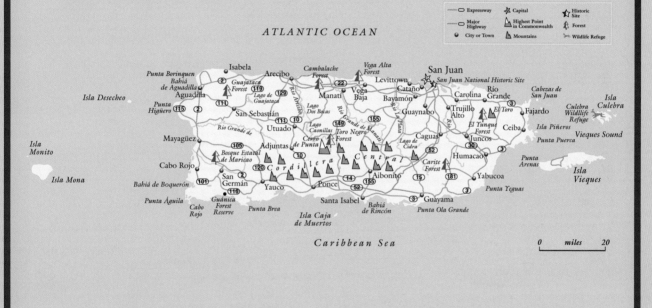

ATLANTIC OCEAN

Punta Borinquen
Bahía
de Aguadilla
Isabela
Arecibo
Cambalache
Forest
Vega Alta
Forest
San Juan
San Juan National Historic Site

Isla Desecheo

Aguadilla
Guajataca
Forest
Manatí
Vega
Baja
Levittown
Cataño
Río
Grande
Cabezas de
San Juan

Punta
Higüero
115
2
119
129
Lago de
Guajataca
Río Arecibo
Lago
Dos Bocas
22
Bayamón
Carolina
El Toro
Fajardo
Culebra
Wildlife
Refuge
Isla
Culebra

San Sebastián
111
10
Utuado
Guaynabo
Trujillo
Alto
El Yunque
Forest

Mayagüez
Río Grande de
Lago
Caonillas
149
Toro Negro
Forest
Caguas
Juncos
Ceiba
Isla Piñeros
Vieques Sound

Isla
Monito

Adjuntas
10
Cerro
de Punta
155
Lago de
Cidra
30
Humacao
Punta
Arenas

Isla Mona

Cabo Rojo
105
Bosque Estatal
de Maricao
Cordillera
Central
52
Carite
Forest
52
181
Isla
Vieques

San
Germán
120
14
Aibonito
15
Yabucoa

Bahía de Boquerón
101
116
Yauco
Ponce
155
52
Punta Yeguas

Punta Águila
Guánica
Forest
Reserve
Santa Isabel
Bahiá
de Rincón
3
Guayama
Punta Ola Grande

Cabo
Rojo
Punta Brea
Isla Caja
de Muertos

Caribbean Sea

0   miles   20

La Borinqueña

words by Manuel Fernández Juncos
music attributed to Félix Astol Artés, as adapted by Ramón Collado

BOOKS

Foley, Erin. *Puerto Rico* (Festivals of the World). New York: Marshall Cavendish Benchmark, 2011.

Pierce Flores, Lisa. *The History of Puerto Rico*. Santa Barbara, CA: Greenwood Press, 2010.

Rigau, Jorge. *Puerto Rico Then and Now*. San Diego, CA: Thunder Bay Press, 2009.

Santiago, Wilfred. *21: The Story of Roberto Clemente*. Seattle, WA: Fantagraphics Books, 2011.

Schwabacher, Martin, and Steve Otfinoski. *Puerto Rico* (Celebrate the States). New York: Marshall Cavendish Benchmark, 2010.

Worth, Richard. *Puerto Rico in American History*. Berkeley Heights, NJ: Enslow, 2007.

WEBSITES

Links to Puerto Rican history, culture, politics, environment, and people:
http://welcome.topuertorico.org

Puerto Rican Culture and History:
http://www.prboriken.com/culture.htm

Puerto Rico Encyclopedia:
http://enciclopediapr.org/ing

U.S. National Park Service:
http://www.nps.gov/state/pr/list.htm

El Yunque National Forest:
http://www.fs.usda.gov/elyunque

Ruth Bjorklund lives on Bainbridge Island, a ferry ride away from Seattle, Washington, and two ferry rides away from Skagway, Alaska.

Richard Hantula is a writer and editor who lives in New York City.

Page numbers in **boldface** are illustrations.

INDEX